Pollinators and Raptors

Written and Illustrated

by

Aadi Agarwal

Published through:

Young Author Academy

 www.youngauthoracademy.com

 youngauthoracademy

 youngauthoracademy

ISBN: 9781079267587

ANIMALS

Pollinators

Bees
Hummingbirds
Kinkajous
Butterflies

Tip: Pollinators are animals that spread pollen to help flowers grow.

Raptors

Peregrine Falcons
Eagles
Owls
Secretary birds
Vultures
Red-tailed Hawks

Tip: To tell if a bird is a raptor, you should check if it has sharp curved claws (also known as talons), a sharp curved beak, eyes in the front of its head, and strong powerful feet.

Pollinators

Bees

A Queen Bee will hatch from its egg in 15 - 16 days, whereas, a worker bee will take up to 21 days. Queen Bees can lay up to 2,000 eggs per day. A drone will hatch in 24 days.

Bees that emerge from an egg can become a Queen, worker or a drone.

A drone is a male bee, whose job is not to collect pollen or nectar, but to mate with the Queen.

Bees have many predators due to their small size. Typical predators include birds, small mammals, reptiles, bigger insects and bears; because they like to eat honey. This means, bears and other big mammals will break a bee's hive.

Bees collect nectar, convert it into honey and then eat it.
Bees pollinate different flowers, according to their habitat.
They pollinate, using the same method as all other
pollinators; which is by taking pollen from one flower and
putting the pollen in another flower.

Hummingbirds

Hummingbirds are the speediest birds in the world. They can fly in all directions; up, down, left, right, forwards, backwards and even upside down.

Although they are extremely speedy, they run out of energy in just 5 minutes. To renew their energy levels, they will drink nectar from heliconia flowers.

The gestation period of a hummingbird is 14 - 16 days, however, if the weather is cold, then the gestation period will be 21 days.

For ruby-necked hummingbirds, the female will sit on the nest for 50-55 minutes every hour.

Female hummingbirds usually lay just 1 egg and rarely lays more than 2 eggs.

Hummingbirds can live for 3 to 5 years.

Some of the predators of hummingbirds are hawks, owls, crows, orioles, roadrunners, grackles, gulls and herons.

Hummingbirds eat flower nectar, tree sap, insects and pollen.

Heliconia flowers are red and yellow, and their stems are long. Hummingbirds are really beautiful; where the male birds are much brighter than the females. This is because the females must stay hidden, to protect their babies.

Kinkajou's

Kinkajous are a small rainforest animal that can be found in Latin American (Mexico), Central American and South American Rainforests.The Kinkajous is the only member of the genus Potos family!

This animal isn't exactly rare, although it is rare for people to see them, because of their strict nocturnal habitat. They are sometimes mistaken for ferrets or monkeys.

The gestation period of a Kinkajous is 112 - 118 days.

The predators of the Kinkajous include foxes, jaguars, jaguarundi, tayras, margays and ocelots.

People are also predators of the Kinkajous, as we hunt them for their meat and fur. Diranul birds of prey are also predators of the Kinkajous. They will take sleeping Kinkajous as they lay in the treetops.

Kinkajous lick the honey from bee hives and at
the same time, will eat insects from the hive,
devour fruits and small mammals.

Kinkajous can live up to 23 years.

Kinkajous usually give birth to only
one baby; rarely two.

Butterflies

Butterflies will pollinate any flower. Some butterflies protect themselves by showing an 'eye mark' on their wings, that frightens their attacker. As most people know, the butterfly evolves from the caterpillar and they typically have beautiful patterns.

Monarch butterfly eggs hatch in between 3 to 5 days. The warmer the weather, the quicker they will hatch.

Predators of the butterfly include spiders, frogs, toads, birds, rats, ants, wasps, parasitic flies, snakes, dragonflies and even monkeys !

Butterflies drink the nectar of flowers with their straw like tongues.

A painted lady butterfly can live for about 12 months; of course, different butterflies will die at different times.

A Monarch butterfly may lay up to 500 eggs at a time.

Peregrine Falcons

You can tell a falcon apart from other raptors; if it has long thin wings, like a boomerang, and a long thin tail with black patches under its eyes. Everyone thinks the cheetah is the fastest animal. This is wrong! The fastest animal is the Peregrine Falcon. A cheetah can run about 112km per hour, but a peregrine falcon can fly up to 389 km per hour. (This is the highest speed ever measured).

A peregrine falcon flies so fast because of gravity. They will fly so high in the sky, tuck in their wings and let themselves fall.

Falcons can easily get killed by great horned owls, golden eagles and other falcons and humans.

Peregrine falcons eat mourning doves, pigeons, shorebirds, waterfowls, ptarmigans, grouse' and small songbirds.

The most common prey for a falcon is the pigeon and these cover up to 99% of the falcons diet. This is just the peregrine falcons' diet. Other falcons have different diets.

Peregrine falcons generally live for 12 - 15 years.
Other falcons' life span is different, as is the same for the number of eggs produced.

The gestation period of a peregrine falcon is about 29-32 days.

Eagles

You can tell an Eagle apart from other Raptors.
They are similar to a hawk,
however, they are just much larger.

A Harpy Eagle is the most powerful eagle in
the world. It lives in rainforests.

The eagle is a major predator; so they will
eat spider monkeys, sloths and many
other small animals.
Fish is also a big part of a bald eagles' diet.

A healthy adult eagle has no natural predators,
but their eggs, chicks, injured hawks and immature
hawks can be prey for other (birds of prey), bears,
wolves and cougars.

They have a slightly light blue-white and
dark-blue pattern on their feathers.

Like most animal species, the lifespan of an
eagle depends on what type the eagle it is.
Bald eagles can live up to 20 years and a
crowned eagle typically can live up to 14 years.

Eagles can lay up to four eggs,
but they usually will lay only two.

The gestation period for an eagle is about 35 days.

Owls

As everyone knows, Owls have huge eyes.
This allows them to see in the dark; all of their other
senses are 100 times more sensitive than human senses.

Most people do not know where an
Owls' ears are located;
they are located on the sides of their heads
but they are hidden by feathers.

Owls do not really have any predators,
but some owls, like burrowing owls,
do; these are foxes, badgers and hawks.

All owls have a diet of insects and small rodents, but
according to their environment, different animals
are added to their diet.

Owls can live up to 20 years, but spotted Eagle Owls
are known to live up to only 10 years.
When in captivity, they can live up to 20 years.

Most owl species typically lay between 2 - 7 eggs.

The gestation period of an Owl is 31 - 32 days.

Secretary Birds

Secretary Birds are the odd raptors; meaning they
don't belong to any such group of raptor,
but they are still considered a raptor.

They use their strong feet for stomping and eating
their prey. They have scales on their legs to protect
themselves from any attack; supposing if,
for instance, a Black Mamba (snake) shall bite.

They have black hairs on their head and have
an orange and yellow face.

A secretary Bird is also known as a Hunter Bird.

The gestation period of the secretary bird is 45 days
and a female secretary bird can lay between
1 - 3 eggs, every two days.

Adult secretary birds have no predators,
but young ones do.
Their predators are crows, ravens, hornbills,
large owls and kites.

Secretary birds can live for 10 -15 years.

Vultures

You can tell a vulture apart from other raptors
if it holds its wings up and wobbles
(shakes), as it soars.

One egg will hatch 6 - 7 days earlier than the
second one. Adult and immature vultures can be
prey for bald eagles, golden eagles, large
red-tailed vultures and great horned owls.

Young vultures are prey for medium sized
mammals such as raccoons and opossums.

All vultures will eat any animal or food waste found dead.
Larger vultures eat small insects and other bird eggs.

Like most animals, vultures have a lifespan according to their species. For instance, a black vulture has a lifespan of 10 years; whereas, a king vulture can live up to 30 years.

Red-Tailed Hawks

You can tell a hawk from other raptors if
it has long, wide wings, soars high and
has a fan-like tail.

A male chanting goshawk will feed their babies in
the nest as the female protects them.
If you get too close to a chanting goshawks' nest,
the female will certainly attack.

The typical gestation of a hawk is unusual,
in that each egg is laid 30 - 48 hours apart.
But for red-tailed hawks, the typical gestation
period is 28 - 30 days, for each egg.

Hawks eat ground dwelling mammals such
as rabbits, voles, mice and other rodents.

A female red-tailed hawk can lay
one to five eggs each year.

Different hawks can live for various amounts of time;
a red-tailed hawk can lives for 25 years.
It is very rare for a hawk to be older than 20 years,
in fact, according to a study of almost 5,200 hawks, only 11
hawks lived for older than 20 years.

ABOUT THE AUTHOR
Aadi Agarwal

Aadi loves to colour, draw and learn.

When not learning about animals that he loves,
Aadi loves to wrestle and have fun with his brother.

Aadi loves to play outdoors and his favourite
sports are tennis and football.

He also loves Science, Art and
English most of all at school.

Aadi chose to write a book about Animals
as he loves to learn about them and their habitats.

He is passionate about saving them and their habitats and
hopes that by learning about them more spreads the
awareness of how amazing they are.